Edition Schott

Alvin Singleton
b. 1940

ARGORU VIII

for Snare Drum
für Kleine Trommel

Edited by/Herausgegben von
Peggy Benkeser

ED 30023
ISMN M-60001-056-1

SCHOTT

www.schott-music.com

Mainz · London · Madrid · New York · Paris · Prague · Tokyo · Toronto
© 2009 SCHOTT MUSIC CORPORATION · Printed in the USA

Preface

ARGORU VIII for snare drum is a daring, even cheeky little piece. It plays with the common notions of what snare drums are supposed to do. For example, it features absolutely deafening silences. It is also decidedly about rhythm on the one hand and about expression on the other, no less so than a popular song might be. Like some strange creature eloquent in only its own language, the snare drum gets worked up but also whispers, gripping the listener in its brutal honesty. The composer is quoted as saying of the work, "I avoided the use of drum rolls, flams and other typical things one associates with snare drumming. Rhythm was my main concentration in the writing of this work." ARGORU VIII was commissioned by Meet The Composer *Commissioning Music/USA* and was written for Peggy Benkeser.

Carman Moore
2009

Vorwort

ARGORU VIII für kleine Trommel ist ein gewagtes, ja sogar freches kleines Stück. Es spielt mit den gängigen Vorstellungen von dem, was für kleine Trommel eigentlich vorgesehen ist. Beispielsweise trägt es Gesichtszüge einer wirklich ohrenbetäubenden Stille. Ferner ist es von Rhythmen einerseits und andererseits von Ausdruck bestimmt, ebensoviel wie ein bekanntes Lied haben könnte. Wortgewandt wie einige fremdartige Kreaturen lediglich in ihrer eigenen Sprache, steigert sich die kleine Trommel, zugleich jedoch flüsternd, und fesselt den Hörer in seiner brutalen Aufrichtigkeit. Der Komponist wird mit folgenden Worten über dieses Werk zitiert: „Ich vermied den Gebrauch von Trommelwirbeln, Doppelschlägen und anderen typischen Dingen, welche man mit dem Spiel auf der kleinen Trommel verbindet. Meine größte Aufmerksamkeit beim Schreiben dieses Stückes galt dem Rhythmus". Argoru VIII wurde von „Meet The Composer Commissioning Music/USA" für Peggy Benkeser in Auftrag gegeben.

Carman Moore
2009
Translation by Thorsten Schlotterbeck

Key:

✖ = rimshot: stick strikes drumhead and rim simultaneously

✎ = quasi rimshot (with fingers)

× = rim click: the butt end of the left stick strikes the rim while
the left palm holds the shoulder of the stick in the center
of the drumhead

A Meet the Composer Commissioning Music/USA commission
for Peggy Benkeser

ARGORU VIII

Alvin Singleton (2002)

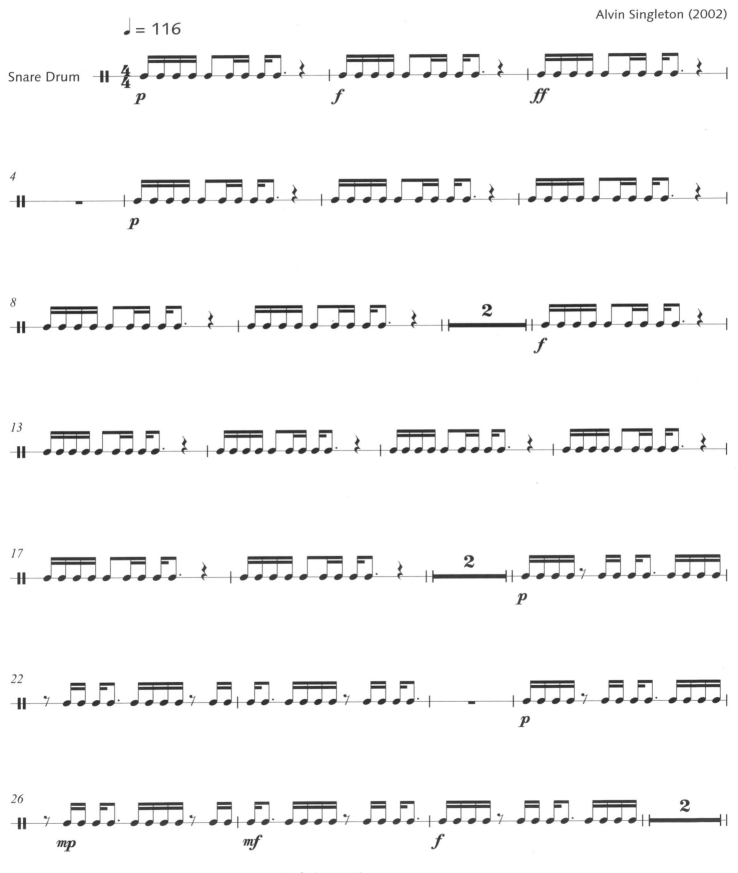

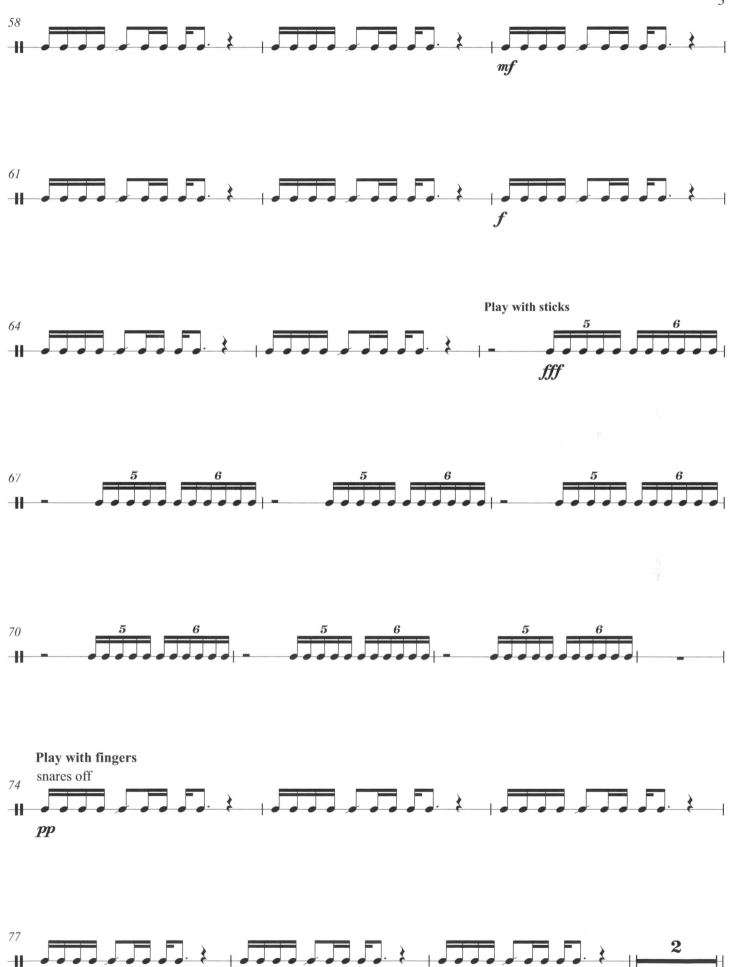

4

Play with sticks
snares on

6   **Play with fingers**
snares off

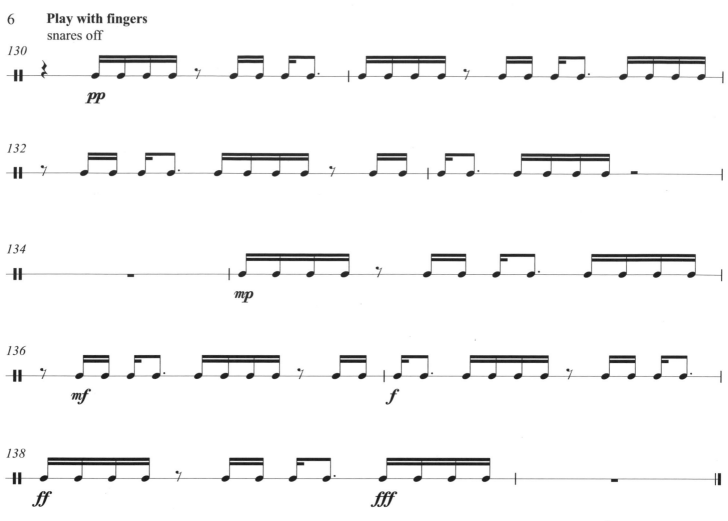

Atlanta, 21 January 2002